The Story of David Zaun

The Story of a victim of OCD

By Edward J Hahnenberg, MA, MA, Ed.S.

© Edward J Hahnenberg, 2016

Introduction

Obsessive-compulsive disorder

OCD, or obsessive-compulsive disorder, can be a serious problem for people. The average age for the onset of OCD, research shows, begins at the around the age of 19, although there are instances where the OCD tendency begins earlier say at age 7 or 8.

What is OCD? As we said above, OCD is an acronym for obsessive-compulsive disorder. I think most people have experienced some form of obsession. It might be the tendency to double check whether the lights in the room have been turned off; or it might be checking to see if the stove in one's kitchen has been turned off. Innocent things like this occur most frequently at any age. There has been a lot of research done about the cause of obsessive-compulsive disorder. My conclusion is that it has a lot has to do with the chemistry inside the brain.

According to the international OCD organization, some of the more common obsessions are the following:

1. **Contamination**: This might be a fear of disease, germs, bodily fluids such as urine or feces, environmental contaminants, dirt, household chemicals, or insufficient hand washing.
2. **Losing control**. This might mean a fear of acting on impulse to harm oneself or

other people, or a fear of acting on impulse, or a fear of violent or horrific images in one's mind, a fear of blurting out obscenities or insults, a fear of stealing things or doing something dishonest.

3. **Harm**: This might be a fear of being responsible for something terrible happening or, a fear of harming others because of not being careful enough.

4. **Obsessions related to perfectionism**: This might manifest itself in a concern about evenness or exactness, or concerned with the need to know or remember something important, or a fear of losing or forgetting important information when throwing something out, or an inability to decide whether to

keep or discard things, or a fear of losing things that are important.

5. **Washing and cleaning**: This might manifest itself in washing hands excessively or in a certain way, excessive showering, bathing, tooth-brushing, grooming ,excessive routines, cleaning household items or other objects excessively, or doing other things to prevent contact with contaminants.

6. **Repetition**: This might be evident in rereading or rewriting something, repeating routine activities such as going in or out of doors, repeating body movements, for example, tapping or touching or blinking, or repeating activities in multiples. Examples of this might be doing something three times

because three is a good number or it's a safe number; maybe doing something 7 times because that's a "lucky number."

7. **Religious obsessions:** This would include fear of damnation or offending God.

It is with this last manifestation of OCD that we begin our story about Dave.

Chapter 1

My acquaintance with David J. Zaun went back to elementary school at St. Frances De Sales Elementary school in Manitowoc, WI. Manitowoc is part of the Door Peninsula well known for its cherry and apple orchards **and** is a popular tourism destination. We had become very close friends even as young kids. Both of us had been raised on fruit farms.

I remember constructing suits of armor made out of tin cans tied together with string.. In the seventh grade, we used to play medieval knights of old. Our swords were made out of wood and we would spar back and forth. It was a fun time in our lives.

About the time of the eighth grade, David's father who was in the military was called upon to go to Germany. He was stationed at Stuttgart . Shortly after the end of World War II there has been a US military presence in Stuttgart that remains to this day.

I didn't like to see him go, and soon forgot about him. Forty years went by before I got a letter from him. He was wondering if I could see him. It just so happens that my wife and I were planning a trip to Germany in the spring of 2005 to see the village of Hahnenberg north of Hanover Germany. I thought it was the village from which my ancestors had come. It turns out that I was wrong.

.   Actually, my ancestors came from Rheinbach, near Cologne. My great great great grandfather was married in that town. Since St. Martin's Catholic Church was destroyed in World War II, and has been rebuilt, there were no baptismal records of his marriage, except in the municipality's courthouse, or at least that's what I was told.

I met Dave in Frankfurt, after having taken a rented auto to visit the village of Hahnenberg, Since he knew English quite well, and I knew no German, we met for dinner at the Hahnenberger Hof in Hahnenberg, Landesbergen.

We both had been in a Catholic seminary….my experience was in St. Mary's Seminary and University in Baltimore,

MD….his in St. George's graduate school of philosophy and theology in Cologne.

During the dinner time, I learned what his life had been like at St. George's .The school was founded in 1926 by the Jesuits, initially to train priests for the Diocese of Limburg. Until 1951 the school was exclusively a seminary, training priest candidates for other German dioceses as well.

David was an only child, born to parents of great faith, Mary and Jacob Zaun. As early as seventh grade, he had wanted to go to the seminary. Through some financial help from the Jesuits, he entered the school in 1955.

The emphasis at the seminary was on becoming saintly. Dave even wrote a prayer in 1959, which he gave to me. I have treasured this prayer ever since.

Prayer of Saintly Commitment

Dear Lord, the all-loving Father of children, look down upon me with that tender and compassionate countenance that has converted so many to your service. Look upon your child as upon one who has begun to understand how totally helpless he is without this eternally endearing gaze. See in my heart, O Eternal Beauty, a desire to serve You completely, totally, with every fiber of my being. Let that approving nod of love so confirm me in dedication to You that I may soon realize that long cherished dream of becoming a saint. Let your understanding Heart, so ready to give other hearts a share in Its love and desires, move you to overcome my fears of not becoming wholly one with You.

You, Who so detest indifference in Your service, come to me daily, and let me see Your divine Face in every conscious act, so that no one, nor anything, will ever shake my desire to sacrifice all for You. Let me share with your loving Mother, Your divine Presence every moment of my life. Let me never be distracted from beholding You in silent peace and love, for I know that my success in Your service depends solely on how closely I am united with You.

Lead me on by Your looks of infinite beauty that I may never lose any of the idealism Your countenance gives me, but may ever fulfill every desire it expresses. May You let me see the compassion in the Face that wept over Jerusalem so that my heart may love souls as Yours eternally does. Grant me never to think any action made in the interests of others too great, and if it be your will, let others see Your kindness and compassion in me.

O most beautiful One, one interest in my life is to love You by leading souls to You. May they learn to love that Face that will be their eternal inheritance. Let my last moments on earth be the holiest and most pleasing to You, and permit me to see You come to take me to Yourself forever with a look so loveable that no earthly bond could restrain me any longer. Then may you wipe every tear from my eyes and grant me the privilege of praising and thanking You and Your mother forever and ever in Your presence and in your sight. Amen.

This life in the seminary he joyfully embraced, and began his six-year training in a typical liberal arts curriculum. During his stay there, since it was a boarding school, he developed friendships with many of his classmates. He particularly liked some of his professors, one who turned out to be a bishop. David was good at sports, engaging in games that the seminary offered such as handball and soccer.

At this early age, Dave began to see sin in thoughts about girls. He would go to confession often, sometimes two or three times a week. I explained to him that thoughts of such a nature are normal and are not sinful. He said that he knew that now but not then.

It was also interesting to hear him talk about this OCD of his as regards his confessors. I don't think that he had priests that understood what he was going through.

We arranged for another meeting the next day. After he left, my wife and I had our first meal in Europe. It included wiener schnitzel, wine, and apple strudel.

That night I began to wonder if there was something in his youth that had created this OCD. I had been retired as a teacher in Michigan for two years. I taught a class in global issues in which I discussed some of the world's diseases.

In the week I spent discussing cancer , heart disease, and malaria, mention was made of one psychological problem that I had noticed in a student of mine. On one of the papers that I had corrected, this junior had erased her name several times. I inquired of her why she had done this. The rest of the paper was typed on a computer, but the heading where her name appeared, was quite thin and showed several erasures.

She confided that she had wanted to have a perfect signature on her paper. So the next day, in all of my four classes, I brought up the question of how many times any of them had checked the lights more than once as they left their room. I asked them to raise their hand if they felt comfortable doing so, and it was interesting to see that quite a number of them had had that experience. I know I had done such a thing. I remember even walking down the sidewalk when I was young trying to avoid stepping on the cracks in the pavement. I brought that up as well to the classes, and saw several nodding in agreement.

Chapter 2

The next morning, I met Dave again at the same restaurant and asked him how his night had been. He said that he was encouraged that I would take the time to talk to him about his OCD.

I asked him to look back into his youth and see if there was something that might have triggered this. He thought a while, and then he said that when he was younger about the first year of primary school, he had gotten into a fight with another student that was a year older than he. It turns out that the other boy had thrown a snowball at him. In response, he had pushed the boy to the ground in the presence of other children. The next day, the older youth threatened to take him to the principal. For some reason, even though Dave said he was bigger and stronger, this threat began to bother him.

Dave had a cousin in the school, who was one year older and in the same class as this boy who threatened him. Dave confided to his cousin what it happened, and his cousin said not to worry about it because he could take care of him if there was any problem. I was surprised that he had not confided this to me before.

I told Dave that I was not a psychiatrist or psychologist, but that maybe because he did not confront this problem straight on, and allowed himself to be taken to the office and suffer the consequences which probably would amount to nothing because the older boy had thrown the snowball first, he might have had more decisiveness about decision-making.

He told me that he would lie in bed at night and try to figure out how to get out of going to recess. He asked his mother for notes that he had a cold or that he was sick. His mother tried to convince him that that was not the way to go, but she did provide a few notes to get through the winter.

Dave told me later on that at a meeting of his grandparents, the boy happened to be related to the family, and when he met the boy, he had forgotten all about it.

Dave said he was so relieved to find out the boy was moving to Canada where he had relatives.

I thought to myself that this failure to make decisions when he was a young boy must have contributed to his inability to make decisions later on in life.

Chapter 3

David related to me that he, as a German, had read about Martin Luther who was also a victim of OCD. He told me that he had a dream about Luther, spending some time with him in his dream. He had asked Luther about his upbringing, and this is what Luther told him. Dave had me understand that this was a dream and not a real occurrence. Luther began in the dream as follows:

"Well, I was born on November 10, 1783, in Eisleben, Germany. I was baptized the next day, the eleventh, and named after the patron saint of that day, St. Martin of Tours. My parents were Hans and Hannah."

Reflecting back to his youth, Luther continued: "My father had had to leave the family farm and seek employment elsewhere. He wound up becoming a copper miner and town councilor. This pleased my mother who had come from a well-placed family in Eisenach. Both my parents were hard-working people. My mother was a religious woman, but she could be very harsh indeed. Once I stole a nut and she beat me until blood flowed."

"My father, too, was a strong disciplinarian. Once my father whipped me so strongly that I ran away. I learned later that he was worried that I would not come back home."

Looking toward me, Luther asked, "I understand that you are the father of children.

What is your feeling about 'sparing the rod and spoiling the child?'"

"I have a mixed record on that issue. I never used a paddle or anything like that. Spanking, yes. I remember thinking, on one occasion, here I was a 210 pound man swatting the behind of my child who was one-fifth my weight. If I couldn't instill discipline some other way, I was not much of a father. So, I pretty much gave up even that."

Luther then offered this thought: "You know, I guess I respected more than loved my parents. It was customary then to beat or whip children, but the memories of my upbringing by my parents are not pleasant ones. I don't think they knew how to keep a right balance between temperament and punishment."

"I am curious about your schooling," asked David. "Please, tell me about it."

Obligingly, Luther reminisced about his education in a series of schools, from the primary grades at Mansfeld, which is south of Eisleben a few miles, to Magdeburg, north of Eisleben, and grammar school in Eisenach until he was eighteen.

"I was told by my schoolmaster that God had prepared me for public office. At Magdeburg, though, I was taught at a school with links to the Brethren of the Common Life. Their hero was the Dutch Augustinian Thomas a Kempis. His book, *The Imitation of Christ*, was well known in the school, and I was deeply influenced by it. Kempis wrote to the ordinary man, encouraging the attainment of salvation by charity and works of mortification."

"I went then," Luther continued, "to the University of Erfurt, after which I was to study law. My father was so pleased that he saved up enough money to buy a copy of *Corpus Juris*, the law of the Roman emperor Justinian. Of course the book was referred to and used in class, and it was in these pages that I came to know the clarity, order, and rationality of the Roman legal system."

"So, at the university, you learned how not only civil law was to be applied, but also how church law worked," Dave added.

"Yes, and I was able to act as my own lawyer in the ecclesiastical proceedings against me by the Pope and his emissaries. In 1505, however, I was caught in a severe thunderstorm, so frightening that I made a vow to St. Anne that, if I were to survive, I would enter a monastery and become a monk."

"I understand that your father was not pleased with your decision."

"My father was especially disturbed by it. He told me that monks were parasites who lived off the offerings of hard-working people;'knavery' he called it."

"He quoted scripture to me:. 'Honor your father' in an attempt to keep me on track to study law. I responded that I felt obligated to my vow to be a monk. He was not impressed, but instead threw up his hands in frustration and muttered something about 'if you can't obey me, how are you going to be faithful to a vow of obedience to the order.'"

"How old were you when you made your vow," Dave asked.

"The incident took place on July 2nd, 1505. I had just been home for a visit and was returning to the university. I was twenty-two at the time."

"You felt you had to keep a vow made in time of great fear?" asked David

"Yes. I felt I was delivered from the storm. However, in a letter to my father, in explanation of my defection from the Old Church, I wrote, 'When I was terror-stricken and overwhelmed by the fear of impending death, I made an involuntary and forced vow.' However, at the time I felt I had to keep my vow. This was not the first time I had received help from heaven in a time of crisis. Two years before, I had a serious accident with a sword, and called out to Mary, Mother of God, for help. My thigh was bleeding so badly, I became quite weak from the loss of so much blood. It took me weeks to recuperate. Also, that same year, one of my closest friends at the university died suddenly. A plague hit the town of Erfurt the year of my vow, so I began to think of death quite seriously."

"What about your mother's view about your becoming a monk?" Dave asked.

"She privately approved. She had always instilled in me the idea that each of us was responsible for our own salvation. If I wanted to be a monk and a priest, she let me know she would be most proud. She told me that I would be assured of salvation by adopting such a life. However, she dutifully followed my father's plan in selecting a young woman to be my bride. This practice was customary in my time."

"I had just passed my master's degree examination in January of 1505, so I had been thinking of the life of a religious for some time. So, I took the thunder and lightning storm in July as a sign from God that I was to be a monk. There were four religious houses in Erfurt: Dominican, Franciscan, Servite, and Augustinian. Two weeks after the storm, I entered the strictest order of the Augustinians, *the Black Cloister*, as a novice. Less than two years later I was ordained deacon, and, on April 4th, 1507, I was ordained a priest in the cathedral."

"Were you happy then?" Dave asked.

"Yes and no."

"What do you mean?" Dave queried.

"As I said my first Mass, I became aware of the gravity of what I was doing, so much so that I couldn't continue."

"Why not?"

"I felt so unworthy to consecrate the bread and wine into the very body and blood of Christ."

"What priest is ever worthy?"

"When I first began to celebrate mass, and to make signs of the cross over the bread and wine, I said: 'Mary, God's mother, how am I plagued with the Mass, and especially with making the sign of the cross.'. The words of consecration terrified me, as did other priests who said them, that they trembled and quaked at the pronouncing of these words: *Hoc est corpus meum,* for they were to pronounce them, *sine ulla hesitatione;* he that stammered, or left out but one word, committed a great sin. Moreover, the words were to be spoken, without any abstraction of thought, in such a way, that only he must hear them that spoke them, and none of the people standing by."

"Don't you think you were being exceptionally harsh on yourself? Priests have celebrated Mass for centuries without the fear you felt?" Dave remembered asking.

"Well, I felt so unworthy at my first Mass, that the assisting monk had to prod me to continue. I don't know what got me through it, except I must have acted blindly because of my fear of not saying the words of consecration correctly and with full attention."

"Did it bother you to say Mass after that?"

"Yes. I used to confess my unworthiness to my confessor, sometimes three times in a day. Once I confessed for six hours."

"My confessor, Johanes Staupitz, tried to ease my fears in confession by binding me to 'blind obedience.' It didn't work because I thought he did not truly understand my fear of having committed sin. . . . besides, his advice at times was rather simple and I could not accept it, because I found arguments that countered it. Other confessors I went to treated me harshly, for they did not have the patience with me that Staupitz had."

Chapter 4

After listening to Dave and his story of his conversation with Luther, I gave him my opinion which I had come to as a teacher.

It is my understanding that abnormal phobias and fears which Luther had forced him to continually analyze in his mind whether he had given full consent to what he thought was serious sin.

The girl's affliction which I had told Dave about sounded very much like what Luther had, except his desire for perfection was in the moral and spiritual realm. Perhaps he felt that if one didn't confess just right or say the Mass in a perfect way, pronouncing each word just so, that he was committing grievous sin."

Dave commented that in his dream about Luther, he had said to him:

"You have come very close to describing my condition. You say that today it is treatable?"

"Yes, but, you did find relief from your hellish life, didn't you?"

"Yes, most certainly. God delivered me with a revelation." With that, he began to sing his most famous hymn , *A Mighty Fortress is Our God.* I felt compelled to join in. His gravelly, deep German bass voice moved me.

"Why could you not accept God's forgiveness? Surely He did not want you to be so afraid of losing your soul. It sounds like you suffered from scrupulosity or obsessive compulsive neurosis . . . a form of depression. Today, this is considered a psychological disorder that is treatable with medication and counseling. I must tell you that modern writers sympathetic to your break with Rome downplay this kind of psychological analysis of your fears."

"That may be true, but I felt this compulsion to confess my sins thoroughly. I would leave confession and realize I had forgotten to explain one circumstance or other . . . so I would return to confession again, without any peace. All I wanted was peace of mind. During the winter I would do extra penance once in a while. Once I lay in the snow, enduring the cold as a form of penance. I became so weak that the monks had to carry me inside. I performed other penances as well. Had it not been for my appointment as a teacher at Wittenberg, I don't know how I could have survived. If I had continued any longer, I would have killed myself with vigils, prayers, reading, and other works."

Dave said that with that revelation, his conversation with the great theologian came to an end

Chapter 5

My wife and I continued on to take a tour of Germany. We rented a car in Hanover and visited Eisenach, the *Bach House*, which was the home of Johann Sebastian Bach. I had done a dissertation on Bach's cantatas and was always very interested in him. Eisenach was also of interest to me because just about a mile away was a huge hill atop which was the Wartburg Castle, southwest of the village. It was the home of St. Elizabeth of Hungary and the place where Martin Luther translated the New Testament of the Bible into German.

Returning to Hanover, Marlene and I went on to Rome by train. It was there that we attended Palm Sunday services on March

20th . Pope John Paul II made one of his last appearances after the Mass, and died on April 2, 2005.

I gave Dave my email and phone number when we parted.

It was about a year later, when I got an email from him. He wanted to discuss more of what he had been through as regards his OCD. I suggested that we Skype each other. He agreed.

Over the next few months, we made contact many times.

Let me tell you , the reader, of some of the struggles Dave went through as a seminarian.

He told me of a time when he was in the seminary, and wore a Roman collar and a cassock. He would go to communion not knowing whether or not he was receiving the body and blood of Christ. This period lasted about six months. It was the most unsettling period of his life. Studying to be a priest and not knowing whether or not Christ was in the Eucharist was his worst nightmare. Later on in life, after he left the seminary, he began to doubt the existence of God.

In his philosophy courses at the seminary, he had studied René Descartes. In his studies of Descartes , he had come across his famous statement:" *Cogito ergo sum*[or "I think therefore I am."

Relying on his philosophical training, Dave was able to establish that he existed himself and that he was not a dream. Moving on from that realization, he asked himself

"How did I get here, who created me, and what was my purpose in life?"

Having been raised in a seminary that taught scholasticism, Dave had read some of the writings of Aristotle. The great philosopher began to think about the infinity of space. Dave had been thinking about Aristotle, who, when he thought about the causality of things, realized that the world that he knew had to have a beginning sometime and somewhere. Aristotle had reasoned that there was motion in the world. The further he thought, the philosopher realized that if he went far back enough in time, he would come to a time when there was still motion in the world. The farthest back in time one could imagine, he reasoned. there was no real beginning. So being the logical philosopher that he was, Aristotle began to take on the idea that motion had no beginning. He called this motion eternal.

In book 11 of his metaphysics, Aristotle goes into great detail explaining this. In this book, which consists of 12 chapters, Aristotle delves into many examples about the question of "being". He draws upon the principle of non-contradiction, saying that a thing cannot be and not be at the same time. As Dave was thinking about Aristotle's argument, he thought about the axioms in geometry. When he took his geometry course in the 10th grade, there were axioms that were accepted without proof. For example, a line was defined as having no beginning and no ending. A segment of a line has a beginning and an ending. If we think of a line in our physical bodies, it has a beginning and an ending.

However David had read some of the more modern philosophers who denied Aristotle's reasoning. So, his mind was in turmoil even after the six-month period when he had doubted the presence of Christ in the Eucharist.

Also during this time, Dave continued to have horrible headaches caused by the fear that whatever he did, he offended God seriously. Dave told me that there were times that he would kneel down by his bed and beg God to relieve him of this phobia. His spiritual director advised him to see a psychiatrist. Seeing nothing else that he could do, Dave went to a psychiatrist for an hour and explained his situation. After an hour went by, the psychiatrist didn't ask any questions. He just sat there listening. Since the session cost $100 an hour, although it was paid for by the spiritual director, Dave left the session no better for the experience. In consultation with his director, Dave said the psychiatrist was not helping and he didn't want him to put any more money into this. Dave said he couldn't afford this continuing path either. I thought to myself Dave never really gave the psychiatrist a chance to work with him.

Dave's OCD became so bad that three months before he was due to graduate, he begged his confessor to leave the seminary and return home. Fortunately, his confessor told him to stay.

As he graduated, Dave learned that he was not recommended to go further in his studies by the Rector. Dave often wondered how that decision was reached. Dave had visited another priest who had told him that despite his problem, he could do anything he wanted with his life because he had the ability and intelligence to do so. Out of the two years that he spent at this seminary, Dave said this was the one priest who understood him better than his confessor. It was this vote of confidence that stayed with him.

Chapter 6

After two years at St. George's graduate school of philosophy and theology in Cologne, Dave left the seminary and sought out a job in teaching. In order to subsidize his living that summer, he was hired on as an orchard manager at an apple farm.

One day while he was out spraying apples, it came to him that he should not go back to the seminary again, even though when he left St. George's, the rector left open to him the option to return.

It was September when he called a local school to see if there was a job there. There were no openings even though the school was just a few miles away. So he called Xavier

College Preparatory School in Aachen about 20 miles away, and the pastor of this parish said to him:

"Not 15 minutes ago, I was in church praying for someone to teach seventh grade in our primary school. I know your parents, so come over and let's discuss this." The pastor's name was Fr. Reinstadt.

Dave asked the farmer to borrow his car to go to see Fr. Reinstadt. Within 15 minutes of meeting with the priest, he was hired.

I asked Dave if he knew what he was getting himself into. Dave said that he did not. He said that the class sizes were ridiculously large. Fifty seventh graders in the morning, and fifty new ones in the afternoon. The pay? Dave said, "about $2500 in your money."

"After the first year, pastor called me in for an interview, and he said that he would have to let me go. I asked him why, although I kind of knew the reason. The numbers of students that I had to deal with were extremely high and I, who was a new teacher, did not have the experience to deal with such large numbers of young people. "

"I asked him for another chance, practically begging, and he thought about it and said he would get back to me. Later that week, he called me and said that after reflection he would give me a second chance."

"I knew this second chance would be my last chance, so I went to a training session for new teachers. One of the most informative sessions was given by a veteran teacher. In the session, he asked how many of us had had problems dealing with young students who get out of control? There were several of us in the group who raised their hands."

"He asked how many of us have had courses in drama." A strange question Dave thought. I had been an actor in the seminary, so I raised my hand. I wasn't the only one by the way.

"He said the key to gaining control from the beginning, is to be an actor. You want them to learn, he said, but the only way is to establish control first."

"When you first meet your new students," he said, "come into the classroom if you are a man, dressed in a black suit and tie. Give directions that are clear and understandable. Take attendance, with assigned seats, and with lesson plans that you actually prepare well. Do not smile for at least two months. Give compliments rarely, do not tell jokes, and show that you are in command."

At this point, I thought to myself, of the success that here in America, a man by the name of Cesar Milan had had great success in dealing with dogs. The man had become known as the "Dog Whisperer" because of his great success in dealing with unruly canines. One of his famous sayings is: "*People just don't realize their dog must respect them as leader of the pack. ... People say I train dogs, but in many ways I train people.*"

Now I am not comparing dogs to people, but as a teacher myself, I thought the presenter of the session with David and his

fellow teachers was doing exactly what Milan
had been doing in the United States from
2004 to 2012.

Chapter 7

David told me that he did exactly as the presenter had said , and his year was an amazing success, and he received compliments from his principal, fellow teachers, and parents. His OCD had abated, and he felt very good about himself and his future.

Money was still a problem, because his salary had only increased by $500 in our currency. Fr. Reinstadt was very pleased and let Dave know about it. It was also a time when expansion of the secondary school was what Fr. Reinstadt had envisioned. A new high school was built. Fr. Reinstadt asked Dave if he would not mind teaching German history in the *Gesamtschule*, or high school.

The pay was better, and Dave said that he would like to do that.

About halfway through the year, as the new high school was being built, the choral director became ill. Dave had an interest in music, having played the piano since he was seven years old. His father had been an organist, as had his mother.

Fr. Reinstadt, who knew of Dave's ability, asked him to fill in. So Dave became both a social studies teacher and music teacher.

After the first year, and having moved into the new *Gesamtschule,* Dave's success as a choral director became apparent to both students, the principal, and the pastor.

The next year, with a new stage and auditorium, Dave was asked to present a choral selection for the school board members, and the pastor. Dave chose a work that would appeal to a German pastor "Nun Danket alle Gott" or "Now Thank we all our God" the lyrics for which were written by Martin Rinkart, and the melody which was written by Johann Cruger .

With a choir of about 50 students, the performance on a Sunday afternoon before a small audience of school board and pastor, was received with surprise and compliments. The pastor was so moved, that he was seen with tears in his eyes by some of the students in the choir.

This success led the students in the school to sign up for choir the next year. His total numbers were well over 150. Dave decided to put on a fall concert. There was no band at the school, so choir was the only music offering that year. Before the first fall concert, a parent of one of the students was an audio technician. He offered to wire the auditorium for stereo sound. A local radio station heard of the choir, and offered to broadcast the concert locally.

When the days came for the concert, two performances were scheduled in November. Seven hundred and fifty parents, relatives, and public attendees filled the auditorium two nights in a row. The students had an opportunity to listen in adjoining classrooms to their own concert. It was quite a thrill for Dave.

The next spring, Dave offered another concert, and the results were the same. The city's Chamber of Commerce asked Dave and his choir to perform at their annual event which honored an outstanding business person in the community.

During this time, David's OCD was in remission. So successful had his program been the first year, that over 300 students applied for music classes. The principal, faced with a decision to allow or not allow so many students to opt for music, decided to limit music classes for those who were in the upper three grades. The scheduling was done by a new superintendent who used a computer program to allocate classes. The result was an unworkable program. For example, Dave found himself with a mis-mash of classes containing some seniors and new students. It did not allow for various choral groups to assemble in the same classes.

So, Dave decided to seek a Masters degree at a local university even though the school year had already started. He resigned his position and moved on to acquire an MA in education. Dave apparently had no problem doing this, because he knew that the choral program would be unworkable.

In a way it was a fortunate move for Dave, because he got to serve his second semester as an assistant to the regional superintendent for Catholic schools.

Chapter 8

Having gained his degree in educational administration, he contacted the superintendent of the school he had resigned from, asking if there was a job available in music. Kind of nervy to do this, he thought, but he gave it a shot. To his surprise, the local superintendent was glad to have him back, this time as a music director for 13-year-olds, or eighth grade in the United States' system.

This year's program was very successful again, and he introduced a new tradition. After each of the concerts that year, all former students were invited to join the choir of 150 in singing Handel's "Hallelujah chorus." Dave was also put in charge of the student newspaper.

In delivering a copy of this newspaper to a neighboring parish, he met his future wife, Hildamar. Dave and Hildamar dated for about a year and got married during Oktoberfest.

That summer before the wedding, another school was looking for a principal. Dave applied and got the job. It was a small Catholic school near Cologne. Dave stayed there as principal for five years. During that time, David's wife gave birth to two children, Dagmar and Conrad.

Since Dave was the sole breadwinner, he decided to look for a job that paid more. Back again he went to the school at which he had been choral director. He was offered more money, and took a job as an assistant principal. This time he did not pursue his musical ability, but instead became head of the theology department.

It was during this time that a new diocese was formed. He and Hildamar met with the first Bishop of the diocese, who later became a Cardinal, in order to express his desire to become a married Deacon.

Over the next few years, Dave returned to the small parochial school where he had been principal, taking on other jobs such as piano tuning and vocal teaching to make ends meet.

There was not enough money to provide for a growing family so Dave decided to add another degree to his resume. While teaching full time at the school that he had been principal, he earned a higher degree in educational administration or educational specialist. In the United States it would be designated as an Ed.S degree.

By this time two more children had become members of the Zaun family, Sabine and Klaus.

Dave spent two years teaching, tuning pianos, and farming. During this time Dave said that his OCD returned with unusual ferocity. He tried to attend Mass every day, and he would get in line for communion, then remember something that had happened the day before. There he was, in line to receive the Eucharist, not knowing what to do because he thought there was some serious sin on his soul. He would reason, in a state of panic that he should continue to go to communion because he had read somewhere that one should not have to expose himself to scandal. This happened so frequently, that the priest told him in confession not to go to Mass daily. "Do whatever gives you peace" It was good advice Dave thought. Dave told me that this reminded him of the poem by Francis Thompson "The Hound of Heaven"

> I fled Him, down the
> nights and down the days;
>   I fled Him, down the
> arches of the years;
> I fled Him, down the
> labyrinthine ways
> of my own mind; and in
> the mist of tears
> I hid from Him, and under
> running laughter.
> Up vistaed hopes I sped;
> And shot, precipitated,
> Adown Titanic glooms of
> chasmèd fears…..

In his realization that there was not enough money to support his growing family, he looked for another school to work at. He thought if he could go to Spain, and find a job there . He applied to the Colegio de la Inmaculada , a Catholic school (grades 1 to 12) run by the Jesuits in Gijon, Spain. To his surprise, he was hired.

One of the reasons he was hired was because of his son Klaus. Klaus had earned a reputation as an excellent young soccer player at Xavier College Preparatory School in Aachen. Klaus was also known for his basketball skills. Colegio de la Inmaculada had an outstanding history of success, with several national championship titles and many players turning professional.

David and his family packed up their goods in their Volkswagen van, and traveled the nearly 1000 miles from Aachen to Gijon. The Jesuits of the new high school were very helpful in providing temporary housing for the Zaun family.

As he school year began, Dave began to wonder why he had taken this long journey with his family. He prayed about it, asking God to give him an answer, and he thought he heard an answer in his mind. He thought he heard God say to him in his subconscious…. "I'm sending the very best."

That was enough for Dave. Over the next year, because of his work in teaching German to his Spanish students, the Jesuit faculty noticed that Dave had administrative skills. The next year they asked him if he would not mind being a administrator in the school. Dave said he would think about it. A discussion with his wife and family led to the conclusion that he would take the job.

As the second year wore on, he began to feel homesick for his native Germany. He informed the administration that he would be leaving and returning to Germany. Dave told me that he realized that this was a rather selfish move, but he missed his country very much.

Sometimes, Dave recounted to me, decisions are made in a kind of a blind way, trusting in God that these feelings he had about Spain had led him to the conclusion that all would work out in the end. His wife Hildamar ,during the past year, had secured a job in public relations at the Colegio de la

Inmaculada as a school promotional person. That would mean giving up that source of income and uprooting their children from a new country and educational system. Hildamar said she was fine with the idea, because she too wanted to return to Germany.

He began calling schools near Cologne that were not necessarily Catholic. He found one school near Cologne that was looking for an assistant principal with a starting salary of €55,000. He thought he had no chance of getting this job, but he applied. The school's name was St. George's international school at Husarenstraße 20, 50997 Köln, Germany.

They took the long journey from Spain to St. George's. He was to be interviewed early in October, after school had already started. There were 34 other applicants for this educational administrative position. He went to the interview, full of hope, but realizing that there were many others who might be better qualified.

On the interview committee was the current principal, one parent, one school board member, and one student. After the interview, he waited for the committee to disperse. The student who was on the interviewing committee saw him sitting there, and said to him "I voted for you." That was a very encouraging sign he thought. Speaking with the principal, he was informed that he would be contacted within the next week.

A week went by and then two weeks, with no contact. Then, just as he was about to give up on this job, he received a phone call from the assistant superintendent, that he should come to sign a contract.

Now the OCD began to kick in again. Should he be involved with public schools? Would the tuition to St. George's be too expensive? He wanted to have his children in a Catholic school if possible.

There was a small Catholic school in Frankfurt about 190 km away, and since religious schools were subsidized by the government the same as public schools, the math added up. Driving that distance would be a problem, however.

Dave mentioned to me that at this time, his wife was pregnant again. Time was of the essence however, so they arrived in Cologne at the end of the month. Finding housing was a bit easier this time for Dave, because he knew prices of homes in the Frankfurt area.

Four more children would be born in the Zaun family. First, Bridget, then Kirsten, and then twin boys Max and Thorsten.

Dave remained as an administrator at St. George's for three years, and then decided to become a teacher. Meanwhile, the mileage was adding up on his newly acquired Volkswagen. As an administrator he had some afterschool duties, monitoring sports activities, writing evaluations for about 40 teachers, and dealing with the normal disciplinary problems. This was really not what he wanted to do. So he requested that he be allowed to teach . This was granted and he spent the next seven years as a teacher at St. George's.

It was during this time of teaching, that the OCD problem became problematic once again. He would stand up in front of the class, and make a comment about some historical figure. In doing so, he would wonder if by saying something about this figure, he would be slandering that person even though the historical person was dead. Crazy fears, but very, very real.

Since his family was in Frankfurt, he had to rent an apartment in Cologne. He had bought a farm outside of Frankfurt. It was a small farm of about 10 hectares, but the farm had an apple orchard on it. During that time he also invested in necessary cultivating equipment, a Deutz tractor, and other implements.

He stayed on as a teacher at St. George's, and, after seven more years, he retired, He related to me that he had found a priest who was very knowledgeable about OCD. He had helped Dave get away from the constant need to confess his imaginary sins by dispensing him from the entirety of confession. The advice was to mention one sin, and stop there. This worked very well for a while, but there were many times, that the compulsion to stop the confession would overwhelm him. If the priest was someone who was not familiar with OCD, he would continue to asked Dave to explain circumstances for his halting his confession, Dave would leave confession with the thought that he had made an unworthy confession. Headaches would ensue, and many times he would refrain from receiving

Communion for a week or more. As time went on however, Dave became more comfortable with the idea that he would not have to confess everything.

During this time, he was able to get a German doctor who prescribed for him a serotonin reuptake inhibitor medication.

I asked him if these two approaches had helped him. He said yes. He had done some reading about Saints in the Catholic Church who had had OCD. One that he mentioned was St. Therese of Lisieux. In her early adolescence she had struggled through an eighteen month long period of scrupulosity.

The *Autobiography of St. Therese of Lisieux*, was a favorite book of Dave's. He quoted to me the following excerpt:

Stimulated by all this unhappiness, my intellectual perceptions developed with surprising rapidity; developed to such a point that in a very short time I felt ill. It was, beyond doubt, the devil's work, this illness which overtook me; Pauline's entry into caramel had enraged him, and he was determined to give his own back for all the loss of influence in which our family was to involve him he didn't reckon with the power of our Blessed Lady, waiting there so calmly in heaven, ready to still the storm before this tiny flower could be overwhelmed by it. It was toward the ends of that year that I was attacked by continual headaches, which worked very painful…. I went on with my schoolwork, and nobody was worried about me. That went on up to the Easter of 1883, in which time my father took Marie and Leonie to Paris, leaving Celine with me in charge of our aunt. My uncle took me out one evening, and talked to me about mama and about old days with a kindliness which made me cry.

I wish I could describe the strange illness of mine. I'm quite persuaded, now, that it was the work of the devil; but for a long time after I got well, I was convinced that I had made myself ill on purpose, and that became a real torment to me. I mentioned this to Marie, who did her best, in the goodness of her heart, to reassure me. I mentioned it in confession, and there again my confessor tried to calm my doubts; it wouldn't have been possible, he said, to make myself as ill as all that nearly by scamming ill. I suppose Almighty God meant to purify and above all to humble me, so he allowed the secret torment of mine to go on right up to the time when I entered Carmel. When I got to Carmel, our spiritual father removed all my scruples just like that; I've never felt the slightest uneasiness about it since.

Dave also told me about another St. Teresa, St. Teresa of Avila. She suffered from the dark night of the soul. In one of her books she mentions that she used to use a feather to regurgitate food that did not agree with her. Dave realized that this was a sign of what we would call today bulimia. Another saint who did the same thing was St. Rose of Lima.

I told Dave that these Saints were probably doing this out of penance, and did not realize that this too was a manifestation of OCD.

Chapter 9

The Problem of breathing

One of the most horrific problems Dave related to me was the act of breathing. Countless times, he would have such a fear of serious sin by simply breathing. His mind would panic as he thought to himself that God would judge him for doubting His existence. Dave would hold his breath, trying desperately to resolve his dilemma. He thought if he didn't breathe, he might be committing suicide. If he did breathe, he didn't know if he was consenting to the thought that God might not exist.

It was probably the worst experience in his struggles with OCD.

Chapter 10

Concluding Thoughts

This whole story about David Zaun, his family, and his struggle with OCD is not a fictional story. Names and dates have been changed to protect those involved. The story is meant to instruct those who do not understand OCD. It might be a confessor, a doctor, or family members who do not understand the hell that obsessive-compulsive disorders can play in a person's life. For some people like St. Therese, it can be over and done within a matter of months or longer. It can however, plague a person for a lifetime. In the case of St. Therese, and in many others afflicted with OCD, the usual way was to ask blind obedience to the confessor. That did help women especially, but certainly not a man like Martin Luther, or well-educated people.

David Zaun's story is a story that is worth reading. For those who know German, the name Zaun, means fence. Those who suffer from OCD are on the fence all the time regarding decisions that must be made.

David left me with one insight that I think is very important. There are actions that are human which result in reflexive, almost automatic acts. However in order to make an action truly human, there must be full realization of what is happening in an act. Decisions of heaven or hell cannot be made in a split second. Serious sin can only be enacted with serious thought. So many of the actions of people, who appear to be criminals, may be those who do not understand what they are doing fully because of their upbringing, their environment, or the culture in whichthey grew up. Who are we to judge what demons, psychological though they may be, engulf those who commit horrendous acts.

Christ says "Do not judge, lest you be judged." Good advice for the ages.